W9-APG-214

READY, SET, PLAY!

SCHOLASTIC

READY SET PLAY!

EDITOR IN CHIEF
Jon White

EDITOR
Hannah Westlake

CONTRIBUTORS
Stephen Ashby, Aiden Dalby,
Ross Hamilton, Carrie Mok,
Dominic Reseigh-Lincoln, Drew Sleep,
Paul Walker-Emig, Mitch Wallace, Josh West

LEAD DESIGNER
Adam Markiewicz

DESIGNERS
Lora Barnes, Andy Downes,
Claire Evison, Ali Innes, Jordan Travers

PRODUCTION
Sarah Bankes, Amy Best

COVER IMAGES
Minecraft © 2017 Microsoft Inc.
All rights reserved.
Splatoon 2 © 2018 Nintendo.
All rights reserved.
Super Mario Odyssey © 2018 Nintendo.
All rights reserved.
Super Lucky's Tale © 2018 PLAYFUL, Corp.
All rights reserved.
Kirby's Adventure © 2018 Nintendo.
All rights reserved.

CREDITS PAGE IMAGE
Yooka-Laylee. Developed by Playtonic
Games. © 2017. Published by Team17.
Team17 are trademarks or registered
trademarks of Team17 Digital Limited.
All other trademarks, copyrights and logos
are property of their respective owners

ISBN 978-1-338-31643-8
10 9 8 7 6 5 4 3 2 1   18 19 20 21 22
Printed in the U.S.A.   40
First printing, September 2018

NOTE TO PARENTS
We have specially selected all the games
in Ready, Set, Play! to appeal to young
gamers and played them ourselves to
ensure they're age-appropriate. These
games will improve reaction speed, build
problem-solving skills, develop imagination
and creativity, and encourage teamwork.
Many of them are even educational, too
(but you might not want to mention that!)

YOOKA-LAYLEE

Explore huge, beautiful worlds with dynamic duo Yooka and Laylee. Help these fun friends defeat enemies and solve some pretty challenging puzzles!

Staying safe and having fun

Video games are the most amazing things ever! Here are some top tips for having fun and staying safe when you're playing. Share them with your friends, too.

1 The games featured in this book are appropriate for you, but always check the rating of any new game before you play it. The ratings are there for a reason, not to stop you from having fun.

2 Talk to a grown-up about your rules for gaming, and ask how long you're allowed to play for.

3 If something happens in a game that you don't understand or don't like, always talk to a grown-up about it.

4 Always be nice to your friends and other players. Don't say or do anything that might make other players feel bad or make them unhappy.

5 If other players are mean or make you sad, stop playing that game for a while. Let your parents know right away.

6 Don't download or install games or apps to any device without checking with the person that owns it first.

7 Tell a grown-up if you see anything that makes you feel unhappy or scared.

8 If you're playing a mobile game always watch out. Be aware of your surroundings to avoid accidents!

9 Remember to take breaks often while playing games, and stop playing immediately if you ever start to feel tired or unwell.

10 Games are even more fun when played with friends, but be nice to your fellow players whatever the outcome. It's only a game!

CONTE

34

28

BLAZERS 94

NTS

◇ Get into

✮✮ Top 5

Which games are right for you? Flowchart p.12-13

104

18

14

42

96

Are you ready?

Games are so much fun! Exploring fantastic worlds with amazing heroes, or battling against your friends is just awesome. But how do you know which games are the best? Well, we're here to help you out! This book is packed with facts, stats, tips, and tricks about the best games EVER!

Ready, Set, Play! will tell you all about the biggest characters in gaming, from Pikachu to Crash Bandicoot. It will help you choose the best games to play with your friends and family locally or online, as well as the coolest games for you to discover on your own.

It doesn't matter which console you play on. If you have an Xbox, PlayStation, Wii U, Switch, 3DS, PC, or even a tablet or smartphone, there are so many great games to enjoy. We've played the biggest and best games on them all, and can't wait to tell you all about them.

So, what are you waiting for? Ready, set, let's play!

106

34

Best games for beginners

Let us show you the ropes

Games are for everyone, whether you like puzzles, stories, or challenges! If you're just starting out, here are some amazing games to try. And if you're already a gaming pro, there are bound to be some you haven't tried yet. Let's get started!

JUST FOR STARTERS

Getting started with gaming

Angry Birds 2
(iOS, Android)

Angry Birds 2 is a simple game. The aim is to knock all the little green pigs down by firing birds at them from a catapult. You press your finger on the bird, pull back, and then let go to fire it off. Easy and lots of fun!

Animal Crossing: Pocket Camp
(iOS, Android)

You can't "fail" in *Animal Crossing* and it's up to you how you spend your time in the game. You can talk to cute animal characters, go fishing, or decorate your community with items you get for trading things you've collected.

Nintendo Labo
(Switch)

Nintendo Labo is a collection of cardboard kits that you can make into incredible toys. You put the Nintendo Switch controllers in them and use them to play fun games. You can make a working cardboard piano, or a robot suit you can use to control a robot on the TV screen.

READY

Super Mario Odyssey (Switch)

Super Mario Odyssey is a fun platformer where you can take control of almost anything in the world by throwing Mario's hat on it. You must collect Power Moons to unlock new levels, and there are plenty of easy levels for beginners.

THE NEXT STEP

Hitting the next level

The LEGO Ninjago Movie Video Game

(PS4, Xbox One, Switch, PC)

The LEGO games are a great way to get into action games. You don't need to learn any difficult button combos and you won't be punished too much if you fail. They are full of funny jokes, too!

Dragon Quest Builders (PS4, Switch)

Dragon Quest Builders has lots of different things to do: fighting enemies, crafting tools, building, and completing quests. It's a great way to get into games that have lots of different types of gameplay.

GETTING HARDER
Testing your gaming skills

Kingdom Hearts III
(PS4, Xbox One)

In *Kingdom Hearts III*, you team up with Disney characters like Donald Duck and Goofy to visit famous worlds from films like *Monsters, Inc.* and *Toy Story*. There's so much to do! You need to manage your inventory, cast magic spells, look after your friends, and beat the bosses.

Mario + Rabbids Kingdom Battle
(Switch)

The controls in *Kingdom Battle* aren't hard, but the strategy is challenging. You have to position all of your characters in the right place and then choose the right actions to out-think the other team and win the game.

Rayman Legends
(PS4, Xbox One, Switch, PC)

This 2-D platformer will really test your reactions. It starts off easy but gets harder and harder as you go on. It's a great way to build up your skills, so keep trying and you'll beat those tricky levels.

Which games are right for you?

Do you love battling your way to first place?

NO → Is exploring more important than winning?

YES → Are you a really competitive gamer?

Mobile games

If gaming on the go is more important to you than anything else, you'll love the portability and choice of mobile games.

Go to p. 44

Flowchart **Which games are right for you?**

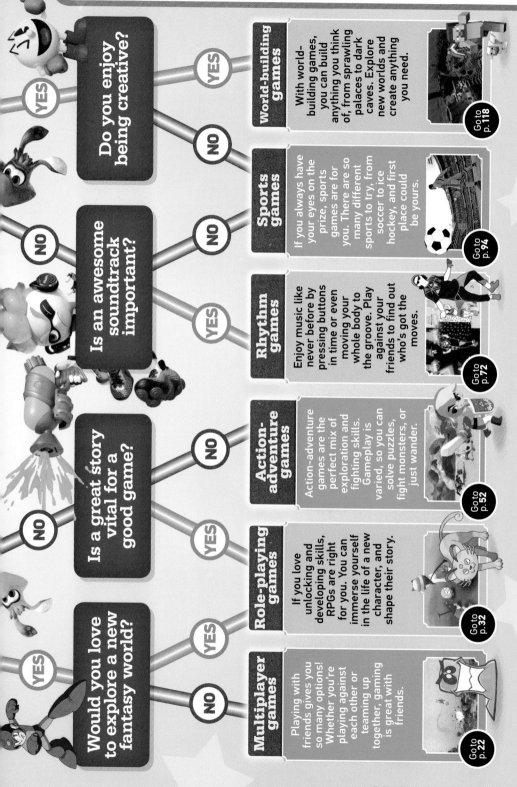

Do you enjoy being creative?

YES → **World-building games**
With world-building games, you can build anything you think of, from sprawling palaces to dark caves. Explore new worlds and create anything you need.
Go to p. 118

Is an awesome soundtrack important?

NO → **Sports games**
If you always have your eyes on the prize, sports games are for you. There are so many different sports to try, from soccer to ice hockey, and first place could be yours.
Go to p. 94

YES → **Rhythm games**
Enjoy music like never before by pressing buttons in time or even moving your whole body to the groove. Play against your friends to find out who's got the moves.
Go to p. 72

Is a great story vital for a good game?

NO → **Action-adventure games**
Action-adventure games are the perfect mix of exploration and fighting skills. Gameplay is varied, so you can solve puzzles, fight monsters, or just wander.
Go to p. 52

YES → **Role-playing games**
If you love unlocking and developing skills, RPGs are right for you. You can immerse yourself in the life of a new character, and shape their story.
Go to p. 32

Would you love to explore a new fantasy world?

NO → **Multiplayer games**
Playing with friends gives you so many options! Whether you're playing against each other or teaming up together, gaming is great with friends.
Go to p. 22

YES

NO

YES

NO

YES

Get to know
Mario
Gaming's biggest star

Mario is a video-game legend. He is best known for his amazing platformers, but he has also been in RPGs, golf games, kart racers, puzzle games, and more.

Mario's TOP 3 superstar sidekicks

Yoshi
Yoshi first appeared as a power-up, but he's since starred in loads of his own games, like *Yoshi's Woolly World*.

2

1

Luigi
Luigi normally appears as Mario's sidekick, but in the ghost-hunting, haunted-house series *Luigi's Mansion*, Luigi is the star.

Toad
Toad proved he can be more than Mario's helper in his puzzle game *Captain Toad's Treasure Tracker*.

3

Latest game:
Super Mario Odyssey
Released:
2017
Bowser has kidnapped Princess Peach and it's up to Mario to save her. Mario has a cool new ability: he can throw his hat onto enemies and take control of them.

Abilities:
★ Jumping skills
★ Special hat powers
★ Kart racing
★ Sports
★ Plumbing
★ Doing flips
★ Breaking bricks

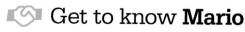

Meowing Mario

Mario games often feature new power-ups. In *Super Mario 3D World*, Mario can get a cat costume to help him climb walls.

FUN FACT

In *Super Mario RPG*, Mario teams up with his longtime rival, Bowser.

First appearance

In *Donkey Kong Jr.*, Mario was a bad guy. He imprisons Donkey Kong and you must save him while playing as Donkey Kong Jr.

Sports star

Mario has shown himself to be a talented sports star in games like *Mario Tennis*, *Mario Golf*, and *Mario Sports Mix*.

Big numbers

Mario has been around for more than 35 years, and has appeared in more than 200 video games!

Mario gets ready to use a feather power-up to leap into the air.

You can create your own cool levels and share them with the world in *Super Mario Maker*.

Get good at

Super Mario Odyssey

Hats off to Mario

Mario's latest adventure on Nintendo Switch is a journey through dazzling worlds. Thanks to his new sidekick, Cappy, the jumping plumber can now possess dozens of creatures, enemies, and objects, too.

Gaming secrets

Mushroom Kingdom returns Finish the main story in *Odyssey* and you'll get a chance to visit the Mushroom Kingdom, Peach's Castle, and your old friend Yoshi!

Tips & Tricks

Explore everywhere

Power Moons are hiding everywhere in *Odyssey*. Leave no stone unturned!

Change your threads

Mario's new outfits don't just look good—they can open up hidden areas.

TOP 3
captures

Bullet Bill

1 Capture one of these explosive missile enemies and you'll be able to fly across huge chasms. Be careful to avoid any obstacles though, since colliding with anything will make you explode.

T-Rex

2 Yes, that's right, with Cappy's help, Mario can possess the king of the dinosaurs. It can smash foes, and clear anything in your path with a swing of its massive tail.

Did you know?

There are a total of 999 Power Moons to find in Super Mario Odyssey, spread across 17 kingdoms.

Uproot

3 Found mainly in the Wooded Kingdom, these plant-like critters can extend their vines into handy stilts. They are perfect for reaching hidden areas or attacking weak spots from below.

Talk to Toad

Having trouble tracking down Power Moons? Hint: Toad will point you in the right direction.

Review the Action Guide

There is a list of Mario's moves, and instructions on how to pull them off.

Get good at

Mario + Rabbids Kingdom Battle

Two crazy worlds collide

We know what you're thinking. Mario and *Rayman's* Rabbid enemies together? In a turn-based strategy game? The gaming mash-up shouldn't work, but it turns out to be a winning combination, and one of the most original games out there.

6aming secret

Ultimate upgrades Beating the main story will grant you access to some secret challenges. Each one you clear will unlock an Ultimate Weapon—one for each character.

Tips & Tricks

Explore the hubs

There are coins hidden everywhere, and more coins means better weapons and abilities.

Try and try again

Some battles will take multiple attempts to beat. Every defeat is a learning experience!

TOP 3 heroes

Mario

1 Who else would it be? Mario is an offensive powerhouse in *Kingdom Battle*, and the ideal hero when you need an aggressive strategy in order to win.

Did you know?

Though the Rabbids originally appeared in the *Rayman* series, Rayman himself is absent here.

Rabbid Peach

2 We're still not quite sure about the selfie-snapping Rabbid imposter dressed as Peach, but on the battlefield, her healing and defensive skills make her extremely valuable to have on your side.

Yoshi

3 Usually known for his flutter jumps and egg-throwing skills, Yoshi is a heavy-weapons specialist here. His arsenal of Rumblebangs is perfect for taking down enemies from a distance.

Take cover

Always look for cover. Leaving yourself exposed could lead to trouble.

Survey the field

Use Tacticam early on to learn the layout of the maps, and make a note of enemy placements.

Top 5
Coolest heroes

The awesome armada

Games feature some of the most unique and awesome characters around. Some may ooze attitude, some are amazingly strong, but all are pretty cool. Here are the best of the best.

1 Sonic
Sonic the Hedgehog series

This speedster blazed onto the Mega Drive in the 1990s. His laid-back attitude, awesome appearance, and high-speed antics means he still reigns supreme 27 years later.

Did you know?

There are three different art styles of Sonic throughout the games: Classic, Modern, and Boom!

2 Pikachu
Pokémon series

When you think *Pokémon* it's hard to *not* think about this iconic electro-mouse. Pikachu's the best thing about the *Pokémon* TV series, too.

3 Link
The Legend of Zelda series

The hero of Hyrule is awesome. He'll gladly volunteer to save the world, he's skilled in almost every ability possible, and he does it all without saying a word.

4 Cuphead (and Mugman)
Cuphead

These ceramic superheroes have to be quick on their feet in this fast-paced "run and gun" indie game. Their cool fire-blasting ability will help you blast your way to the bosses.

5 Crash Bandicoot
Crash Bandicoot series

Crash is the unlikely hero, the underdog—and everyone *loves* an underdog. Stopping the evil genius Doctor Neo Cortex is this goofy bandicoot's mission.

ASK A PRO

Every video game character has different abilities—from splashing colorful ink to smashing wooden crates—and you might find it hard to get used to the variety of controls. By playing around with different characters, and being patient, you'll quickly find your favorite hero and power combination.

Get into
Multiplayer games

It's fun playing with friends

Some of your best gaming moments will be playing with friends. Whether playing against each other or teaming up together, multiplayer gaming is a great way of sharing your hobby.

This huge donkey is just one of the crazy weapons you can use in *Worms W.M.D.*

Retro roots

Karate Champ Early arcade fighters of the 1980s like *Karate Champ* were the first chance many people had to compete against their friends.

Overcooked is always trying to up the chaos levels. Watch out for icy floors as you dash around.

QUICK TIPS

Play safe
In *Worms W.M.D*, try to finish your turn with your worm in a safe place.

Hold tight
If you hold the punch button in *Gang Beasts*, you are able to grab other players.

TOP 3 GAMES

Worms W.M.D

1 You take control of a team of worms, and can play against friends online or locally. You take turns using silly weapons, like an exploding sheep, to try and get each other's worms and win the game.

★ ★

Gang Beasts

2 In this funny fighting game, you and your friends move around trying to control colorful characters and throw them over the edge of the level. You won't mind if you lose, though, because you'll be laughing so much.

★ ★

Overcooked

3 Embark on a cooking adventure with your friends! Prepare, cook, and serve complicated meals for your demanding customers, but watch out for slippery floors and sneaky rats. This game isn't about coming first, it's about working together despite the cooking chaos.

Versus mode

If you're really competitive, try out *Overcooked*'s Versus mode. You can try out all the arenas you've unlocked.

👍 If you liked these, try out

Mario + Rabbids Kingdom Battle

LEGO Marvel Super Heroes 2

Kirby Star Allies

Get good at
LEGO Marvel
Super Heroes 2

A time-traveling adventure

You get to be Spider-Man, Black Panther, and lots of other cool superheroes in this amazing LEGO game. Your superhero team travels through time to visit Ancient Egypt, Medieval England, and the Wild West to beat Kang the Conqueror.

Gaming secret

Take a selfie As Ms. Marvel, you can take selfies with other heroes. You can even replace the pictures on the in-game billboards with Ms. Marvel's best selfies and admire your work!

Tips & Tricks

Smash it all
Smash up everything in the level to collect as many studs as you possibly can.

Replay
Replay levels with heroes with different abilities if you want to collect all the game's studs.

TOP 3
Superheroes

Spider-Man

1 This amazing web-slinging hero is awesome. Spider-Man is able to climb up walls, has a super jump, and can shoot webs at the bad guys.

Rocket Raccoon

2 This feisty little raccoon is a member of the Guardians of the Galaxy. He carries a cool laser rifle with him to take out any enemies.

Did you know?

Up to four people can play LEGO Marvel Super Heroes 2 together as a team of superheroes.

Captain America

3 Captain America has loads of incredible powers. He has a double jump and wall jump, he can deflect bullets with his shield, and he can throw his shield to activate shield switches.

Special attack

When a blue color hovers above your head, switch characters to perform a cool double attack.

Fly high

Use a flying character in order to explore high areas for hidden collectibles.

Get good at

Rocket League: Collector's Edition

Giving soccer a supercharge

Take the sport of soccer and swap the players with rocket-powered cars, and you've got *Rocket League*. As a beginner, you can have so much fun speeding after the ball with friends. Get good, though, and you'll discover a strategic sports game that you'll always love.

Gaming secret

Back in time Enter the famous Konami Code during startup and it'll take you to the intro screen for *Rocket League*'s predecessor, *Supersonic Acrobatic Rocket-Powered Battle-Cars.*

Tips & Tricks

Fueled up
Try to make sure you've always got some boost in the tank for when you really need it.

Flying high
Practice using your boost to fly into the sky to get to those high balls before anyone else.

TOP 3 reasons to keep playing

New modes

1 New stuff is always being added, including new modes like the ice hockey and basketball-style versions of *Rocket League*. They give you new ways to play and test your skills.

Tournaments

2 The addition of tournaments to *Rocket League* allows you to compete against a group of friends locally or online. If you don't win, then there's always next time.

Did you know?

Rocket League has sold over six million copies and been enjoyed by 40 million players.

Customization

3 There are so many cool ways to customize your car, and regular updates add even more. From WWE to Hot Wheels-themed items, there's something for everyone in the Garage.

Stay back

One player from your team should always hang back to stop counterattacks from your opponents.

Get the goalie

Knocking into the other team's goalie when your teammate is about to shoot is a great tactic.

READY, SET, PLAY!

Get to know
Sonic
The blue blur

This lightning-fast, blue hedgehog is the speediest hero in video gaming. Sonic uses his jumping Spin Attack and speed to defeat enemies, collect rings, and save cute animals from evil Dr Eggman.

FUN FACT

In early designs for Sonic, he was a rabbit. After Sega decided on a hedgehog, an early name suggestion was Mr. Needlemouse.

Sonic's TOP 3 spin-offs

1

Sonic & All-Stars Racing Transformed

This kart-racer is packed with characters from *Sonic* and Sega games, and your car can even transform into a plane.

Mario & Sonic at the Olympic Games

Compete against Mario in events like the long jump, volleyball, and more.

2

Sonic Spinball

In this pinball spin-off, Sonic curls up and becomes the pinball that you play with.

3

LATEST GAME
Sonic Forces
RELEASE DATE:
2017

This game mixes classic 2-D platforming with modern 3-D platforming. You switch between playing as Sonic and a new hero that you create yourself.

Abilities:
- ◆ Supersonic speed
- ◆ Witty comebacks
- ◆ Spin Attack
- ◆ Spin Dash
- ◆ Racing
- ◆ Sports
- ◆ Pinball

Faithful friends

Sonic is often joined on his adventures by friends like the flying fox Tails, Knuckles the echidna, and Amy Rose the hedgehog.

Super Sonic

By collecting Chaos Emeralds, Sonic can transform into Super Sonic. He turns yellow, runs faster, jumps higher, and can't be hurt.

Power-ups

Sonic can collect power-ups, like an electric shield with a double jump ability, or power sneakers that help him to run even faster.

Superstar

Sonic isn't just a video-game star. He has also had his very own television and comic book series.

The trusty Tails is often by Sonic's side to give him a helping hand.

Sonic runs from an orca in his first 3-D title, *Sonic Adventure*.

RE   520
E 1° 57 "09
GS   70

00:56:16
05

Get good at
Sonic Mania

Going old-school

Using the retro style of *Sonic* classics, *Sonic Mania* mixes the best of past and present. The game includes remixed versions of famous *Sonic* levels and brand-new ones. With lightning-fast platforming and cool new bosses, *Sonic Mania* is really exciting.

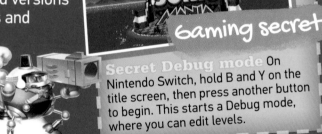

6aming secret

Secret Debug mode On Nintendo Switch, hold B and Y on the title screen, then press another button to begin. This starts a Debug mode, where you can edit levels.

Tips & Tricks

Drop dash

Hold the jump button after jumping, and Sonic will do a drop dash when he hits the ground.

Explore

Look around you for hidden routes to find power-ups, extra lives, and secrets.

TOP 3 zones

Mirage Saloon Zone

1 This stage has a side-scrolling shooter section, loads of Wild West-themed gimmicks, and even a runaway train.

Green Hill Zone

2 The most famous zone in *Sonic* history is the Green Hill Zone, so it's great to revisit it in *Sonic Mania*. It has had a few tweaks, including a great new boss battle.

Did you know?

The team that made *Sonic Mania* started out as fans making their own *Sonic* games and mods for fun.

Stardust Speedway Zone

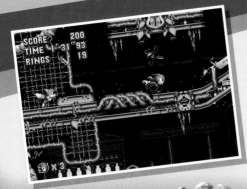

3 Visit past and future versions of the Stardust Speedway Zone in *Sonic Mania*. The past version is full of plants and pulleys, and the future version has cool, high-tech gadgets.

Watch and learn

Bosses attack in patterns, so if you watch carefully, you'll be able to predict what's coming next.

Ring collector

Collect as many rings as you can. If you have rings, you won't get a game over when you are hit.

Get into RPGs

Level-up your gaming knowledge

In role-playing games (RPGs), you take on the role of the character in the story, and make decisions for them. You can often level-up to unlock new skills and become more powerful as you play.

Retro roots

Pokémon Red and Pokémon Blue
The first *Pokémon* game on the Game Boy was a big success in 1996, and series is still going strong to this day.

Each area in *Golf Story* has its own style and is full of secrets to seek out and uncover.

Pokémon Sun and *Pokémon Moon* both have their own special Pokémon you can find only in that version.

Superstar Saga has a Minion Quest mode where Bowser's Minions are trying to save their boss.

QUICK TIPS

Have a mixed team
If you only have fire type Pokémon and must fight a water type, you'll be stuck.

Watch the wind
There's an arrow that shows where the wind is blowing in *Golf Story*. Use it to plan your shot.

TOP 3 GAMES

Pokémon Ultra Sun and Pokémon Ultra Moon

1 Catch Pokémon and use them to battle other Pokémon trainers on your quest to become the best. Your Pokémon get stronger and learn new moves as they progress.

★★★★★★★★★★★★★★★★★★★★★★★★★★★★

Golf Story

2 *Golf Story* is a great intro to RPGs. It mixes classic RPG stuff like quests and leveling-up, with golf. There's no need to worry about confusing battle systems—just have fun playing golf instead.

★★★★★★★★★★★★★★★★★★★★★★★★★★★★

Mario & Luigi: Superstar Saga + Bowser's Minions

3 Mario and Luigi travel to the Beanbean Kingdom to get back Princess Peach's stolen voice. Battles are turn-based. That means that you and the enemy take turns picking moves.

X marks the spot
Look out for hidden paths in *Superstar Saga*. There are platforming challenges inside.

👍 If you liked these, try out
Super Mario RPG
....
Kingdom Hearts III
....
Okamiden

Get to know Steve

He can do it all

Steve may have a pretty regular name, but *Minecraft's* hero is a special guy—he can dig mines, build huge castles, fight zombies, craft tools, make potions, cook food, and grow crops.

FUN FACT

The name "Steve" was originally suggested as a joke by *Minecraft's* developers.

Steve's TOP 3 challenges

1 Visit the Nether

Build yourself a portal out of Obsidian, and you can visit the dangerous Nether world. Bring strong weapons and armor.

2 Beat the Dragon

Destroy all the end crystals, since these will heal the Ender Dragon. Then start the tough task of taking it down.

3 Defeat the Wither

Build a T with four blocks of Soul Sand. Put three Wither Skulls on top, and it will turn into a tough Wither boss.

Latest game:
Minecraft

Released:
2011

Minecraft is an amazing world made of blocks. You can collect resources, craft tools, fight monsters, and build almost anything you can imagine.

Abilities:
- Mining
- Sword fighting
- Building
- Crafting
- Farming
- Enchanting
- Cooking

Super Steve
Steve can punch out blocks of wood using his bare hands, but we'd suggest crafting an ax to get it done quicker.

Switch it up
You can change the color of Steve's skin, or get new costumes and characters to play as.

Take a hike
Steve walks at 4.37 blocks per second. That means you can walk a total of 5,181 blocks in one *Minecraft* day.

King of hearts
Steve has a health bar of ten hearts. Each heart takes two hits, so you can take a total of 20 hits.

An exploding Creeper is a scary sight, especially when it's close to something amazing you've built.

Being able to build with your friends is one of the best things about *Minecraft*.

Get good at
Minecraft
Master all things 'Craft!

Minecraft is amazing because it can be as big as your imagination—which is pretty huge if you've got some massive ideas. The possibilities are endless. To help you become the ultimate builder, here are some of the best tips for master crafting.

Gaming secret

Halloween spookiness
Every October 31, *Minecraft* has a makeover. Bats appear at light level six (rather than three), and Zombies and Skeletons bring jack-o'-lanterns.

Tips & Tricks

Try Creative mode first
Before you fight Creepers and Zombies, test out the game's mechanics.

Spawn at your bed
There's a spawn point at the center of your world, but if you build a bed and sleep in it, that's your new spawn point.

TOP 4
Aquatic update mobs

Phantoms

1 Phantoms are a new mob, and can be a little scary. They fly high up in the air, and attack users who haven't slept in a while!

Dolphins

2 *Minecraft* recently updated with water and oceans to explore. These little mammals are a cute new feature. They can even lead you to treasure-filled shipwrecks.

Did you know?

The very first version of *Minecraft* was designed and built in just six days. A lot has changed since then!

Turtles

3 These water mobs can be found throughout water-based biomes, and will usually be seen making nests on watery shorelines. They're really friendly, too!

Fish

4 If you're going to give *Minecraft's* oceans, lakes, and rivers an overhaul, then you have to sort out those fish, too! Fish are both a mob and an item for cooking with.

A quick shelter

If in Survival and far from home, dig three blocks into the ground, and place a block over you.

Signs and ladders

Signs and ladders can be used to stop the flow of water *and* lava. Not bad for a bit of wood!

Did you know?
Iconic Creepers were made when *Minecraft's* creator tried to code a pig and it went wrong!

Every world is randomly generated. This means it's built right there and then, and is unique to you.

Timeline

NOVEMBER, 2011
THE 1.0 UPDATE
The first post-beta update added enchanting, brewing, breeding, Hardcode mode, and The End.

OCTOBER 25, 2012
PRETTY SCARY UPDATE
This update added in a ton of monster-based mobs, the Wither boss, beacons, and anvils.

SEPTEMBER 2, 2015
THE BOUNTIFUL UPDATE
One of *Minecraft's* biggest changes, 1.8 brought new blocks and updated Survival mode.

2018
THE UPDATE AQUATIC
The 1.14 update brings new water physics, structures, blocks, items, and mobs.

Minecraft can be a place to design by yourself, or you can share a server with friends and build together.

There are some awesome multiplayer modes in *Minecraft: Console Edition*.

ASK A PRO

When you're playing in Survival mode, have plenty of torches on hand. They light up dark places, but also have lots of other secret uses. They create temporary pockets of air underwater, can break stacks of gravel/sand, and you can even build right on top of them as well.

Did you know?

Once every 10,000 times you play, the title screen will misspell its own name to read "Minceraft."

Q&A

How many modes are there?

There are two main ones: Creative (which gives you an infinite inventory, removes all dangers, and enables you to float), and Survival (where you need to mine and craft all your items).

Can I use mods?

Yes, you can use mods (downloadable patches that change how the game works or looks) but only with the PC version. Mods don't work on mobile or console versions of *Minecraft*.

The latest update, 1.14, is called the Update Aquatic, and it brings a big, water-based makeover to the game.

Get good at
Minecraft: Story Mode

Crafting your own adventure

Playing as Jesse, go on some exciting and dangerous adventures with new friends you meet in a *Minecraft*-themed world. It's not a sandbox game anymore. The choices you make on your adventures change how the story plays out.

Gaming secret

A hidden banner Head toward Gabriel's keynote stand at EnderCon to find a hidden Mojang banner. It's a shout out to Mojang, the developer who made the original *Minecraft*.

Tips & Tricks

Quicktime events
In QTE sections where you fight mobs, wait until the enemies are yellow or you will miss.

Be ready
A QTE section could be coming at any moment, so stay on your toes.

TOP 3 epic moments

The Wither Storm

1 In the first episode of *Minecraft: Story Mode*, a giant monster called a Wither Storm is created. It's your job to find a way to stop it.

The reveal

2 There's a great twist in *Story Mode* where you find out that a character is not who you thought they were. We won't spoil the surprise!

Did you know?

There are eight episodes in the first season of *Story Mode*, and five in the second season.

The New Order

3 The moment where Jesse and friends become legends when they are made the New Order of the Stone is a cool reward for all your hard work.

Explore

Take your time to explore, and you will find some cool extra bits of dialogue.

Your choice

There are no wrong choices, just different ones, so don't worry too much about your decisions.

Get good at
Super Lucky's Tale

The fantastic fox

In this 3-D platformer, you get to visit magical lands on your quest to save Lucky's sister from the final boss, Jinx. You will collect coins, battle enemies, meet colorful characters, and face challenges on your journey.

Gaming secret

Tunnel Dweller There is a secret achievement in the game for burrowing 32,000 feet (10,000 meters), so make sure you spend plenty of time tunneling underground.

Tips & Tricks

Clover collector
Collect all of the letters that spell out "Lucky" in a level and you will get a clover.

Look for Secrets
There are Secrets hidden everywhere, so try smashing and jumping on everything you come across.

TOP 3 villains

General Buttons & Colonel Fluffy

1 There is a whole team of cat villains to beat in the game, including the tiny General Buttons and the huge Colonel Fluffy, who have their own pirate ship.

Tess

2 A clever cat called Tess is an inventor who likes to come up with crazy gadgets. Her inventions aren't always reliable, so watch out for explosions!

Did you know?

You need to collect 300 coins in a level in *Super Lucky's Tale* to be rewarded with a clover.

Lady Meowmalade

3 All this fancy kitty cares about is how good she looks. She's taken over the town of Spookington and you must save the town and its cute residents.

Air Spin

Use Lucky's spin attack in the air for longer hangtime. This can help avoid enemies and hazards.

Get more lives

If you're low on lives, just go back to an easy level to collect some more.

Get into Mobile games

Gaming fun on the go

Thanks to mobile gaming, we can game wherever we go. From simple puzzles to beautiful stories, there's a mobile game for everyone.

You can charge up energy and unleash special power-ups in *Arkanoid vs Space Invaders*.

Retro roots

0015

Snake II The *Snake* games were some of the first that you could play on cell phones. Everyone was trying to get the highest score on their cell phone.

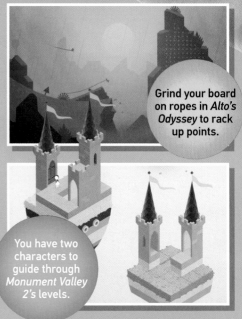

Grind your board on ropes in *Alto's Odyssey* to rack up points.

You have two characters to guide through *Monument Valley 2*'s levels.

QUICK TIPS

Wall ride
You can ride on walls in order to keep your run going and reach high ledges in *Alto's Odyssey*.

Place your bow
Tap the screen to put your bow and arrow there while in attack mode in *Arkanoid vs Space Invaders 2*.

TOP 3 GAMES

Monument Valley 2
iOS, Android

1 *Monument Valley 2* is a clever puzzle game where you can twist and turn the level to open new paths for your character to walk down. It's got great music and beautiful looks.

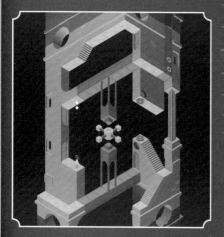

Arkanoid vs Space Invaders 2 **iOS, Android**

2 In *Arkanoid vs Space Invaders 2*, you control a ship flying along the bottom of the screen. You have to bounce a ball off your ship in order to take out blocks and the space invaders.

Alto's Odyssey
iOS, Android

3 *Alto's Odyssey* is a cool sandboarding game, where you slide through amazing landscapes that are different every time you play. The game is as relaxing to explore as it is fun to play.

Take it easy
Be patient and enjoy playing with the world in *Monument Valley*, and you will surely get to the solution.

👍 If you liked these, try out

Harry Potter: Hogwarts Mystery

Animal Crossing: Pocket Camp

Sonic the Hedgehog Classic

Get good at

Stardew Valley

Have fun farming

A t the beginning of *Stardew Valley*, you take over an old, overgrown farm. Your job is to make it the most successful farm possible. You can plant crops, take care of animals, craft tools, and explore caves for metal.

Gaming secret

Hidden Hat Shop Head to the southwest corner of the map and you'll find a shop where you can buy cool hats for your character.

Tips & Tricks

Find secrets

If you see wiggly worms in the ground, something is buried there. Use your hoe to dig it up.

Build a silo

Build a silo early on and all the grass you cut will be collected as hay.

TOP 3
cool things to do

Exploring Caves

1 If you want action, you can go exploring in caves where you can find enemies to fight and metal ore to collect.

Make friends

2 Head to Pelican Town and make friends. You can even get married and your new partner will help on the farm.

Did you know?
There are over 30 local residents for you to get to know in Pelican Town.

Go fish

3 If you're looking for something relaxing to do, take a seat by the river and spend some time fishing. See how many fish you can catch.

Happy birthday

Do you want villagers to like you? Just give them a nice present on their birthday.

Go to Bed

If you stay up too late, your character will fall asleep and you will lose some gold.

Get good at
Yo-Kai Watch 2

Meet some friendly spirits

Some naughty spirits called "Yo-Kai" are causing trouble, and it's your job to stop them. You can use your special Yo-Kai Watch to catch your own team of cool Yo-Kai, and then use them to battle the bad Yo-Kai.

Old Springdale

Gaming secret

Five-Star Coin Go to the second counter in the Lambert Post Office in Springdale and enter the code "friends!" at #2 counter and you'll get a free Five-Star Coin.

Tips & Tricks

Forget side quests
The main quest will teach you how to play the game, so stick with that from the beginning.

Tribe mates
Put two Yo-Kai from the same tribe next to each other on the battle wheel for a stat boost.

TOP3
Yo-Kai

Jibanyan
1 This cute Yo-Kai is the first one you get in the game. Thanks to its cute looks, Jibanyan has become the mascot for the series.

Whisper
2 This friendly ghost Yo-Kai doesn't fight. Instead, he stays by your side to give advice. He likes to show off how much he knows about Yo-Kai.

Lie-in Heart
3 Evolving from Lie-in, this is an ice-based Yo-Kai with abilities like Lightning Slash, Frost, Lion Blade, and Biding Time.

Did you know?
There are more than 650 Yo-Kai to befriend in the Yo-Kai Watch series.

Have a healer
Make sure you have a healer in your team for when your Yo-Kai get hurt.

Use elements
Pay attention to the elements. Fire is weak against water, but strong against ice.

Get good at
Knack 2
Action, platforming, and puzzles

Knack is an action-platforming star with a cool special ability. He can collect debris, and use it to grow as tall as a building. He can get rid of the clutter to shrink again so that he can fit through small holes.

Gaming secret

Got the knack? If you can collect 70 out of the 143 medals in the game, then you will receive a cool gold trophy called You've Got the Knack.

Tips & Tricks

Shield parry
Hold L1 to raise your shield just before an attack lands in order to parry it.

Multi punch
Make sure you unlock the multi punch from the skill tree. It's a powerful attack.

TOP 3 new features

Cool moves

1 Knack has learned some new tricks since his first game. He can do punch-and-kick combos, dodges, body slams, and other special moves.

Platforming paradise

2 The first *Knack* game didn't have much platforming. But in *Knack 2*, there are loads of fun platforming sections so you can experiment with Knack's jumping skills.

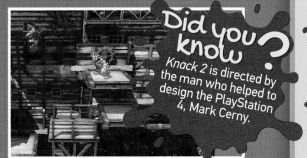

Did you know?

Knack 2 is directed by the man who helped to design the PlayStation 4, Mark Cerny.

Co-op combinations

3 When you are playing in co-op mode with a friend, you can team up to do cool double-team moves. For example, if you hit your buddy, they will fire out bullets.

Build a converter

The energy converter lets you turn yellow crystals into relic energy so you can upgrade your skills faster.

Get into
Adventure games

Gameplay and top worlds

Action-adventure games mix the wonder of exploring cool new worlds with the excitement of testing your gaming skills. They can include all kinds of gameplay.

There are loads of cool Skylanders to choose from to battle against the bad guys.

Retro roots

The Legend of Zelda: Ocarina of Time This gaming classic had loads of cool new ideas. Lots of games use the enemy lock-on idea from *Ocarina of Time*.

There are puzzles to solve in *Ittle Dew 2's* dungeons, as well as enemies to beat.

QUICK TIPS

Get cooking
Cooking yourself some tasty food in *Breath of the Wild* will give you a stat boost.

Check your element
Fire Skylanders are weak against water, air is stronger against earth, and so on.

TOP 3 GAMES

The Legend of Zelda: Breath of the Wild

1 *Breath of the Wild* is set in a massive, open world, and you are free to go wherever you want. There are monsters to fight, puzzles to solve, cool characters to meet, and loads of secrets to discover.

★ ★ ★ ★ ★ ★ ★ ★ ★ ★ ★ ★ ★ ★ ★ ★ ★ ★

Skylanders: Imaginators

2 You can put *Skylanders* toys onto a Portal of Power, and then play as that figure in the game. You can switch between Skylanders with different powers as you battle the bad guys and try to save the world.

★ ★ ★ ★ ★ ★ ★ ★ ★ ★ ★ ★ ★ ★ ★ ★ ★ ★

Ittle Dew 2

3 *Ittle Dew 2* is a cute action-adventure where you explore a magical island to find what you need to build a raft and escape. There are dungeons to explore, bosses to beat, and lots of jokes.

Save your weapons

Weapons wear out in *Breath of the Wild*, so make sure you save your best ones for toughest enemies.

👍 If you liked these, try out

Lightseekers

....

LEGO City Undercover

....

Spyro Reignited Trilogy

Play with Friends
LOCALLY

Sharing games with friends is lots of fun. These great local multiplayer games will have you all laughing at funny moments, marveling at close wins, and trying not be sore losers.

Mario Kart 8 Deluxe (Nintendo Switch)

One of the things that makes this kart racer so much fun is the items. You and your friends can hit each other with turtle shells, drop slippery banana peels, and more!

VS.

Co-op

Did you know?

Snipperclips has 45 levels. You can get another 40 with the *Snipperclips Plus* DLC.

Overcooked
(PS4, Xbox One, Switch, PC)

In *Overcooked*, you and your friends play as a team of chefs. You must work together to cook as many dishes as you can in crazy kitchens set on icebergs, trucks, and pirate ships.

Snipperclips—Cut It Out, Together!
(Nintendo Switch)

In this two-player game, you and your friend play as two cute little characters. You can cut each other into different shapes to help you solve puzzles together.

Team

CO-OP MODE

This game mode is all about working together to achieve a goal. It's short for "cooperative."

Team Sonic Racing (Xbox One, PC, PS4, Switch)

Team Sonic Racing features co-op like never before. Select a team with your friends and work together in each race, sharing items and speed bonuses.

Co-op

LEGO Marvel Super Heroes 2
(PS4, Xbox One, Switch, PC)

You and your friends can choose from loads of cool super heroes to play as, each with their own special superpowers. You fight enemies, find hidden collectibles, and solve LEGO building puzzles together.

Co-op

Play with Friends

ONLINE

Y̲ou don't even need to be in the same room to play video games with your friends. Jump online and battle with or against your buddies in amazing multiplayer games, co-op adventures, and exciting one vs. one duels.

Super Smash Bros.
(Wii U, 3DS)

Your favorite characters are all here and ready to battle it out in *Super Smash Bros.*. Pick your fighter and you're ready to show the world what a battling champion looks like.

TEAM MODE

Team is a game mode in which you and others join together to win against another team.

VS.

Rocket League
(PS4, Xbox One, Switch, PC)

Rocket League is a bit like soccer, but with rocket-powered cars instead of players. You and your pals can go online to play in three-on-three, two-on-two, or one-on-one matches against other players, or each other.

VS. MODE

Vs. mode allows all the players involved to compete against each other.

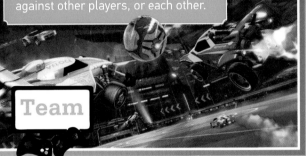

Team

Did you know?
There are over 70 awesome weapons you can unlock in *Splatoon 2*.

Splatoon 2
(Nintendo Switch)

In *Splatoon 2*, two teams of four go up against each other in the messiest shooter in gaming. To win, you must cover the stage in more paint that the other team.

Team

FIFA 18
(PS4, Xbox One, Switch, PC)

Pick your favorite team and play against your friends online to see who comes out on top. When you're done competing against each other, you switch to online co-op mode.

VS.

Gang Beasts
(PS4, PC)

Gang Beasts lets you choose a colorful and wobbly fighter to help you battle for dominance against other gamers. The environments are almost as dangerous as the other players, so watch out!

VS.

Get to know

Pikachu

We choose you!

There are hundreds of Pokémon, but none can rival the charm of Pikachu. The lightning-shooting monster was one of the original 151 Pokémon, and has since become the series's mascot.

FUN FACT

Pikachu was a mascot for the Japanese national soccer team when they played in the FIFA World Cup™ in 2014.

Pikachu's TOP 3 spin-off appearances

1 Hey You, Pikachu!

This N64 game is a real *Pokémon* oddity, and had a microphone attachment that let you talk to Pikachu!

2 Super Smash Bros.

Pikachu's speed, mobility, and powerful electric attacks make it a great choice in Nintendo's crazy fighting series.

3 Detective Pikachu

Not content with battling foes and leveling up, this game has Pikachu solving mysteries too. What can't Pikachu do?

LATEST GAME:
Detective Pikachu
Release Date:
2018

This spin-off adventure for 3DS stars a talking Pikachu with an eye for a clue. It's a new career for Pikachu, too—no more fighting Pokémon; it's time to fight crime!

Abilities:
- Thunderbolt
- Quick Attack
- Spark
- Agility
- Discharge
- Thunder Wave
- Tail Whip

Pikachu parents

Breeding and hatching a Pikachu egg will give you a Pichu, while using a Thunder Stone on Pikachu will evolve it into a Raichu.

Friends from the start

Pikachu appears in the very first episode of the *Pokémon* anime, and quickly becomes hero Ash Ketchum's best pal.

Time icon

In 1999, Pika-fever was at its highest, and *Time* magazine even voted Pikachu as its second-best person of the year.

Catch 'em all

Though it's appeared in every core game, Pikachu couldn't be caught in *Pokémon Black, White, Black 2* or *White 2*.

Pikachu flies through the air, and gives Mario a skull bash in *Super Smash Bros.*

You can catch Pikachu in *Pokémon Sun and Moon*, or it'll evolve from a Pichu.

Get good at

Pokémon Ultra Sun & Ultra Moon

Welcome back to Alola!

Grab your friends and set out on another epic *Pokémon* voyage! *Ultra Sun* and *Ultra Moon* pack in even more challenging quests, fierce battles, fun activities, and—of course—new Pokémon. They are the most complete *Pokémon* adventures yet.

Gaming secret

The ultimate test If you are able to beat the Elite Four and the Poni Gauntlet, you will be able to visit the Battle Tree, which is where the most powerful trainers lie in wait.

Tips & Tricks

Know your types
Some Alolan Pokémon have changed their typing, so know their strengths and weaknesses.

The right moves
Don't overlook moves that boost your stats and weaken enemies—they can be crucial in battle.

TOP 3
Alolan forms

Exeggutor

1 Alolan Exeggutor's big grin is definitely catching. With its long, palm-tree neck and coconut-swinging tail, it's really made the most of the region's tropical climate.

Sandslash

2 This hardy Pokémon has swapped its type from Ground to Ice and Steel to adapt to its chilly new mountain home. Even the spikes on its back have frozen solid.

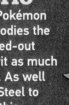

Did you know?
You can scan QR codes with the 3DS camera to receive a number of special Pokémon as gifts.

Dugtrio

3 No Pokémon embodies the chilled-out Alolan spirit as much as Dugtrio. As well as adding Steel to its typing, this burrowing monster has a selection of new hairdos.

Fill the Pokédex

It seems obvious, but the more *Pokémon* data you have, the greater the benefits will be!

Return to explore

Revisit previous areas. Your new abilities could unlock secrets you missed the first time around.

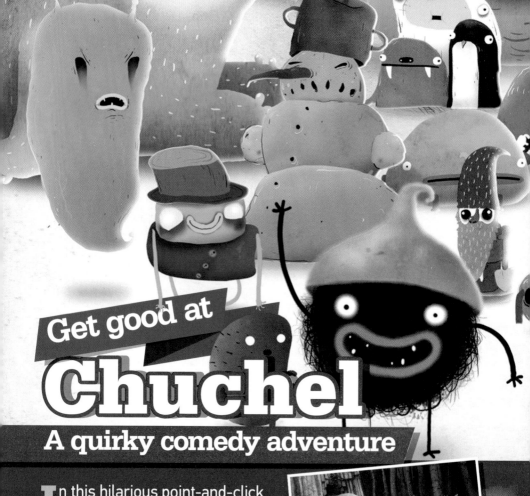

Get good at
Chuchel
A quirky comedy adventure

I n this hilarious point-and-click comedy adventure, you control a small furry creature named Chuchel who is trying to chase down a delicious cherry. The game's crazy characters, strange surprises, and Chuchel's funny tantrums will keep you entertained the whole way through.

6aming secret

Guest appearance Look through a telescope at the end of *Samorost 3* and you can see Chuchel chasing a cherry in space.

Tips & Tricks

Click everything
Chuchel is more about comedy than puzzles, so clicking on everything will normally get you through.

Take a moment
Some puzzles have a set pattern. Take the time to learn them.

TOP 3
characters

Did you know?
Chuchel means "hairy bunch" in Czech, the native language of developer Amanita Design.

Chuchel
1 It's no surprise that the star of the show is the best character. Chuchel's expressions are so great that they are always guaranteed to get a laugh.

Kekel
2 This funny little creature is a rival for Chuchel's beloved cherry, but sometimes the duo have to work together to get hold of it.

The snail
3 When you meet the snail, it transforms into an arcade where you can play versions of *Pac-Man*, *Space Invaders*, and *Tetris*. It's one of the game's many strange surprises.

Sign of success
A sign will pop up if you are struggling. Click on it to get a helpful tip.

Play for laughs
Even if you know the solution to a puzzle, try clicking on other stuff to see what funny things might happen.

Brain-training games

Games that get you thinking

Games can be a great workout for your brain. Your problem-solving, organization, and task-managing skills can all be improved by playing some of these fun and smart titles.

Did you know?
Sega has owned the *Puyo Puyo* series since 1998. The games have since been developed by Sonic Team.

1 Overcooked

To win in *Overcooked*, you need to be quick, organized, and to communicate with your friends while watching out for the level's different challenges. It really tests your ability to multitask.

2 Human Resource Machine

This logic-based puzzler teaches the basics of coding. You are tasked with organizing a series of commands to create instructions for the workers.

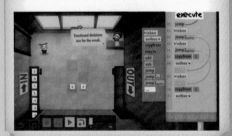

3 Puyo Puyo Tetris

You'll need to think quickly in this puzzle game, as it changes mode every couple of minutes! It'll switch between making lines to grouping colorful Puyos, so make sure that you're on top of both games at once.

Snipperclips

4

You control Snip and Clip and alter their shapes to complete a variety of puzzles and objectives. It's fun on your own, but better with a friend.

Snake Pass

Unlike other platformer games, *Snake Pass* makes you think about physics and how snakes actually move. You will have to master the odd controls while solving puzzles and making it across some very difficult levels.

5

ASK A PRO

Having problem with a level or puzzle? Trying over and over, and failing, can get frustrating. Take a break from the game, grab a snack, and come back to it after a couple of minutes. You might see a solution that wasn't there before!

Get good at

The LEGO Ninjago Movie Video Game

Play the movie

Play through key parts from the movie as your favorite characters. It has the look and feel of past LEGO games, but with some cool new features that make it fresh, like Spinjitzu attacks.

D 9 T Z 3 9

Gaming secret

The secret character There is one character who is only available by entering a cheat code. Press Start in Free mode, go to Enter Code, and type D9TZ39.

Tips & Tricks

Combo time
Bigger combos in combat not only look sweet, but will earn you more studs.

Backtrack
Finding certain items in a level will require powers you unlock later in the game.

TOP 3
coolest characters

Skylor

1 She can take down enemies from far away with her crossbow. Skylor is also one of the few characters to know Universal Spinjitzu, making her an ideal choice for unlocking collectibles.

Master Wu

2 The mentor of the six Ninjas and master of elements doesn't look bad for 167 years old. He wields his Nin-Jo staff and moves around like someone much younger.

Did you know?

There are eight locations to explore, all from the movie. Each one has challenges to test your skills.

Lloyd

3 The only one of the Secret Ninja Force to be a Master Builder, Lloyd is as skilled at building as he is in combat. He's great for any situation.

Don't fear death

You have unlimited lives, so don't be afraid to make risky jumps.

Acronix

This character can sprint, making the races in each level a bit easier.

Get good at

Splatoon 2

Splat your way to success

The goal in *Splatoon 2* is for you and your team to cover the stage in more paint than the other team. You can splat other players to slow them down and send them back to the start!

Gaming secret

Get a wave On the right side of Inkopolis Square, you can see Off the Hook in their studio recording the news. Press ZR to look in first-person mode and they will see you and wave.

Tips & Tricks

Hide in ink
When you are standing on your own colored ink, you can dive into it to hide from the other team.

Paint to win
Remember that painting the stage is more important than splatting the other team.

TOP 3
special weapons

Ink Armor
1 This special weapon covers everyone in your team in ink armor. If you time it right, this is really great for pushing forward as a team and then taking ground from the enemy.

Baller
2 With the Baller, your character gets in a speedy hamster ball that can roll up walls. It explodes in a big splat of paint when it runs out.

Did you know?
Splatoon has regular "Splatfests" where you choose a side, like ketchup vs. mayo, and see who wins.

Bomb Launcher
3 You can throw loads of bombs in a row with this special weapon. If the other team is in one area, the Bomb Launcher is great for splatting them all at once.

Single-player mode
The single-player mode is a great way of getting to know all of the game's different weapons.

Super Jump
Don't forget to use your Super Jump ability to leap to a teammate when you're in trouble.

Get good at
Lightseekers

The champion of fighters

Like *Skylanders*, *Lightseekers* is a fun toys-to-life experience. This one links your mobile device with cool action figures that light up, vibrate and even say stuff. Play through a cool role-playing adventure or battle against some of your friends using official trading cards.

Gaming secret

Secret scanning In addition to using your device's camera on *Lightseekers* trading cards, you can also scan the packaging, boxes, and store displays for some awesome in-game surprises.

Tips & Tricks

Lights, camera, action!

Scan *Lightseekers* cards into the game using your mobile device's camera to unlock cool extras.

Powering up

Be sure to equip new abilities as you earn them to become even stronger in battle.

TOP 3 heroes

Boulder

1 Harnessing the power of magma, crystal and earth, Boulder is one seriously rocking Everok. He swings a smoldering Molten Blade and uses his Crystalcore to take fiery flight.

Did you know?

If you shake a Lightseekers figure or turn it upside down, it will get mad and tell you to stop!

Zyrus

2 Looking like an evil purple ninja, this Noxin hero relies more on dark magic than martial arts. His creepy tools include a Leeching Scimitar and one bat-shaped Grimglider.

Sgt. Ironbark

3 What do you get when you cross a walking redwood tree with a hardened military sergeant? An awesome evergreen hero who can do a lot of damage in a fight. Sgt. Ironbark is super tough.

Rock solid

Add Lightstones to weapons and armor to increase stats like attack, damage, and vitality.

Let's chat

Talk to as many characters as possible. They'll give you quests that can be completed for rewards.

Get into Rhythm games

Move to the beat

Enjoy music in a whole new way with rhythm games. You play along with the music, either by timing your button presses to the beat, or by dancing along using motion controls.

You can dance together with friends in *Just Dance 2018*.

Retro roots

Dance Dance Revolution This early rhythm hit came with a dance mat. You play by stepping on the right arrows on the mat in time with the music.

Check and turn the signal to the left!

PaRappa is always rapping, even when he is learning to drive!

QUICK TIPS

Take your time
Use your first time on a rhythm game to get to know the songs. Don't worry about your score.

Ramp it up
Start with the Easy difficulty songs on *Just Dance 2018* to learn some basic moves.

TOP 3 GAMES

PaRappa the Rapper Remastered

1 You play as a cute rapping dog called PaRappa. He meets lots of funny characters who teach him new raps as he dances along. You must time your button presses for PaRappa to get the raps right.

Runner3

2 In *Runner3*, the character you control is always running forward. You have to time your jumps and slides in time with the game's music in order to avoid the dangers in your way. This game is the perfect mix of platforming and music.

Just Dance 2018

3 *Just Dance 2018* is full of hit songs for you to dance to. Using motion controllers or a phone with the *Just Dance* app, you copy the moves of the dancers. The more moves you get right, the more points you get.

Listen up

Don't rely on the visuals to get your timing right. Make sure you always listen to the music.

If you liked these, try out

LEGO Rock Band

....

Theatrhythm Final Fantasy

....

Pianista

READY, SET, PLAY! **73**

Get to know
Crash Bandicoot

An icon returns

This PlayStation legend has been gone for a while, but now Crash Bandicoot is back. The goofy hero has starred in 3-D platformers, his own racing series, and party games.

FUN FACT

Before his return in *N. Sane Trilogy*, Crash made a surprise appearance as a playable character in *Skylanders: Imaginators*.

Crash Bandicoot's TOP 3 games

1

Crash Bandicoot N. Sane Trilogy

It doesn't get any better than having three great games in one. That puts the *N. Sane Trilogy* at the top of the pile.

Crash Team Racing

In this fun racer, you can play as Crash Bandicoot, Doctor Neo Cortex, Coco Bandicoot, and many more.

2

Crash Bandicoot: The Huge Adventure

3

This game proves that Crash Bandicoot can do 2-D platforming just as well as he can 3-D platforming.

Latest game:
Crash Bandicoot N. Sane Trilogy

Released:
2017

Updated versions of the first three adventures in one: *Crash Bandicoot*, *Crash Bandicoot 2: Cortex Strikes Back*, and *Crash Bandicoot: Warped*.

Abilities:
- Cyclone attack
- Jumping skills
- Crash Dash
- Racing
- Scuba diving
- Climbing

In a spin

Crash Bandicoot's most famous ability is his cyclone spin attack that he uses to take out enemies.

Spirit guide

Aku Aku is a spirit who helps guide Crash. If Crash finds three Aku Aku masks, he becomes invincible for a short time.

Cortex's creation

Crash was a normal bandicoot until he was evolved by the evil Doctor Neo Cortex. Crash started fighting to stop Cortex from taking over the world.

All-arounder

In his racing game spin-offs, Crash is an all-arounder, with decent stats for speed, acceleration, and turning.

Crash is looking cool while riding his motorbike down the road.

Crash slides toward danger. Let's hope he doesn't get squished!

Dingo Diner
5¢ SODA

Get good at

Crash Bandicoot N. Sane Trilogy

Three in one

The *N. Sane Trilogy* is a collection of Crash Bandicoot's first three platforming adventures. The colorful critter explores a fun world, collecting Wumpa fruits and using his cyclone attack to take out enemies on his way to stopping the evil Doctor Neo Cortex.

Gaming secret

Hot Coco On the Road Crash level, crash into the alien-head sign to the left of the road. You'll be taken to a secret jetski level called Hot Coco.

Tips & Tricks

Watch your shadow
You can see where you will land after a jump by looking at your shadow.

Easy extra lives
If you're running out of lives, simply go back to an easy level and collect some more.

TOP 3
N. Sane moments

Playing as Coco

1 You can unlock Coco Bandicoot and play with her in all three games. It's cool to be able to play through all the games with a new character.

Motorway madness

2 There are some exciting vehicle sections in *Crash Bandicoot: Warped*, where you get to ride a speedy motorbike and fly a plane.

Did you know?

One of the original ideas for Crash's character was a wombat called Willy the Wombat.

Rampage

3 When you collect three Aku Aku masks, you become invincible for a short time. It's super fun to let loose and smash everything in your way.

Try the D-pad

Try using the D-pad for 2-D platforming parts. You might find it much easier.

Keep trying

The second and third games will get easier if you keep messing up.

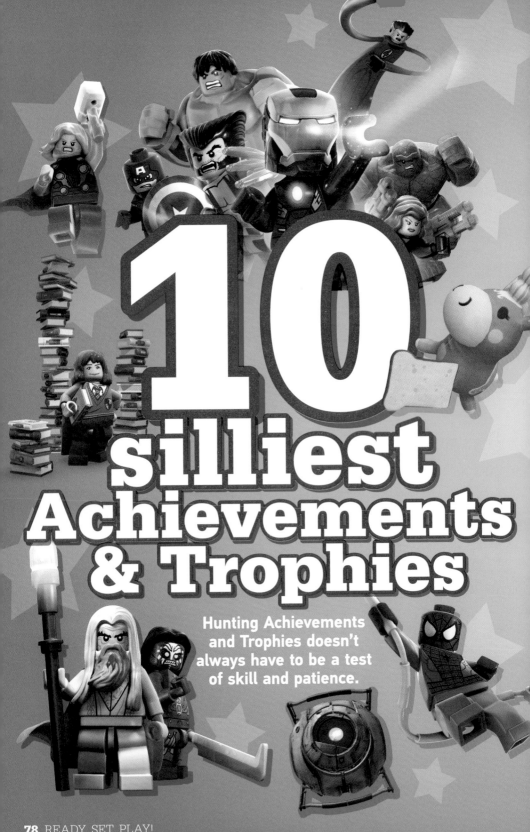

10
silliest
Achievements
& Trophies

Hunting Achievements and Trophies doesn't always have to be a test of skill and patience.

The Simpsons Game is full of really silly Achievements and Trophies.

1 Lots of Ideas for Trophies
Undertale

Coming up with ideas for Trophies is easy, right? *Undertale* developer Toby Fox certainly thought so. This one can be gained by picking up just one item. His next great idea? Get two items. By the time you've picked up four, you'll have unlocked Help Me, I'm Out of Ideas.

2 Press START to Play
The Simpsons Game

While there are plenty of silly Achievements to be found in *The Simpsons Game*, this is definitely *the best*. Dubbed the "easiest achievement ever," all you have to do is boot up the game and press START to Play. That's it!

3 Don't I Know You?
LEGO Marvel Super Heroes

Actor Chris Evans is famous for portraying Captain America on screen, but he also had a small stint as the Human Torch in *Fantastic Four*. Bring the two together in LEGO *Marvel Super Heroes*, and you'll unlock Don't I Know You? as a sly reference to the movies.

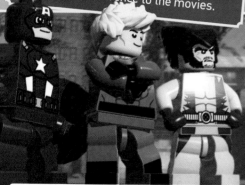

4 Joy-rye-der
I Am Bread

This simulation game, which turns you into a living slice of bread, has its fair share of silly Trophies, but this is probably our favorite. You'll need to get through the maze-like garden and find a way into the car to get it, starting the vehicle using your bread-like prowess.

LEGO *Marvel Super Heroes* puts some of Marvel's most serious heroes in some really ridiculous situations.

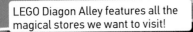
LEGO Diagon Alley features all the magical stores we want to visit!

5 Solid Snape
LEGO Harry Potter: Years 1–4

If you play as Professor Snape—Harry Potter's least favorite Hogwarts' teacher—and stick him in a barrel, you'll unlock the Solid Snape Achievement. There are plenty of barrels hidden around the world, but we recommend visiting Diagon Alley.

6 Beat Yourself
FIFA 08

The primary objective in any game of soccer is to put the ball in the back of your opponent's goal. Scoring one own goal is a mistake a team can come back from, scoring two is . . . well, a little unheard of. In fact, two own goals will put this mark of shame on your account forever.

Maybe the movies were wrong and you really can walk into Mordor after all!

7 One Does Not Simply . . .
LEGO The Lord of the Rings

Boromir claimed "one does not simply walk into Mordor" in *The Lord of the Rings: The Fellowship of the Ring*. Well, prove him wrong. Use any character and walk directly into Mordor's Cirith Ungol to earn this silly reward.

8 In the Dark
TMNT 1989 Arcade

Games don't typically reward you for paying zero attention to what is happening, but earning In the Dark is as easy as falling into an open manhole five times. Do it once, it's an accident. Do it five times and, well, it starts to get a bit silly!

Portal 2 will really test your puzzle-solving skills—unless you refuse to move!

9 You Made Your Point!
Portal 2

In Chapter Eight of *Portal 2* you will encounter a test chamber, with a *super* easy puzzle inside. But, instead of completing it, just stand there. Stand there and wait as Wheatley, your robot companion, gets increasingly exasperated that you can't follow simple instructions. It's pretty funny, and it'll get you a fun Trophy too!

10 Not a Portal Reference
'Splosion Man

Underrated platformer *'Splosion Man* has you blowing yourself up to bounce across platforms and literally explode your way through levels. Grabbing all 47 collectible slices of cake in the game will get you this Achievement. It's a reference to the phrase "The cake is a lie," which was made famous in *Portal*.

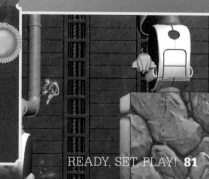

Get good at

Super Mario Run

Tap and go!

Mario's smartphone adventure takes him through all kinds of new challenges as he tries to save Princess Peach. Mario runs across the screen automatically, so all you have to do is tap at the right time to jump over enemies and collect coins!

Gaming secret

Secret world If you collect every pink, purple, and black coin in the game, you can buy a pipe for your Kingdom that will open secret new stages!

Tips & Tricks

Slow it down

If you stand on a red pause block, the clock will stop. Take your time and plan ahead.

Collect the coins

Collect pink coins to unlock more levels and move on to the harder purple and black coins.

TOP 3
game modes

World Tour

1 Take on the challenging levels created by Nintendo in this mode. Collecting the five pink coins in each level will make it tougher the next time you play.

Remix 10

2 Take on ten fast and frantic levels in quick succession to collect rainbow coins and unlock new buildings for your kingdom— and eventually save the princess.

Did you know?

Mario's brother, Luigi, and his dinosaur friend, Yoshi, are both unlockable characters. Play as them for different jump styles.

Toad Rally

3 In this mode, all that matters is looking good! Pull off cool jumps, collect coins, and show off your skills to collect a crowd of Toads. Beat your friends' times for the best rewards.

Unlock characters

Save up your Toads from Toad Rally to buy houses in your Kingdom. Some will unlock new characters.

Tap and hold

Tapping quickly will make Mario small jump. Tap and hold to jump higher, and tap while in the air to do a spin move.

Get good at
Nintendo Labo

Create and play

Labo lets you build devices from cardboard—called Toy-Cons—and use them to play a series of games. You don't need glue or scissors to start building, everything you need is included with the game.

The next step

Labo Robot Once you've mastered Toy-Cons, check out the Labo Robot Kit. Build the suit, control a giant robot, and destroy any buildings.

Tips & Tricks

Parental help
Toy-Cons such as the fishing rod can get complicated—having a parent around can help.

Be careful
While the Toy-Cons are sturdy, they are still made out of cardboard and can break.

TOP 3 Toy-Cons

Motorbike

1 Joy-Cons are inserted into each side of the handlebar, and when tilted left or right, the character in the game will steer in that direction.

Did you know?

28 sheets of cardboard are included in the Labo Variety Kit, as well as an extra sheet for customizing.

Piano

2 With no strings, the piano features a whole octave, and it works! Add blocks to the top to change the sound from a piano to other things, like cat noises.

RC Car

3 This is the easiest to assemble, so it's best to start with. You move the car around using the Switch's touchscreen, which makes the Joy-Cons vibrate.

Nintendo will help

If your cardboard does tear or gets worn down, you can ask Nintendo for a replacement sheet.

Extra functions

The RC Car Toy-Con can follow your hand around using a built-in camera.

Get good at LEGO Worlds

Build your own empire!

If you love the freedom of sandbox games and the humor and creativity of LEGO games, you'll love LEGO *Worlds*. If you can imagine it, you can build it in LEGO *Worlds*. We've compiled all the best tips for building your own wonderland.

Gaming secret

The 200 Gold Brick reward
Collect 200 Gold Bricks and you'll unlock the PUG-Z/Test Rocket. It costs 150,000 studs, and enables you to fly around your world super quick!

Tips & Tricks

Use the Discovery Tool
Scan anything with this tool so you'll have the plans to build it later.

Study the beacons
Beacons on the map lead to different things. Gold ones lead to treasure, red to dungeons, and so on.

TOP 3
vehicles

Did you know?

The game's "worlds" are randomly generated, so every single one you start is completely new and unique to you.

Hot Rod

1 What better way to make your way around the randomly generated lands of LEGO *Worlds* than an old school car? It can be found in the Dusty Dunes and Playful Prairies biomes.

Cole's Earth Driller

2 Want to start carving a mark into that randomly made brick world that you've just been dropped into? Then you need the four-wheeled wonder that is Cole's Earth Driller!

Creator Lawnmower

3 Part item and part vehicle, the Creator Lawnmower is one of your go-to pieces of gear for turning wild patches of blocky ground into smooth lines, ready for further building. Found in Creator Towns.

Collect Gold Bricks

Gold Bricks are rare, but collect 50 of them to create even larger worlds, or 100 to become a Master Builder.

Go questing

Quests are really important, so be sure to follow those green beacons to find the ones nearby.

Get to know
Link

Meet the hero of Hyrule

Link has come a long way since his humble beginnings in *The Legend of Zelda* on the NES. He has saved kingdoms, slayed monsters, and conquered evil time and time again.

FUN FACT

Link made his motor-racing debut in *Mario Kart 8 Deluxe*, where he's available as a bonus character.

Link's TOP 3 companions

1 Princess Zelda

Zelda is a powerful warrior and manages to rule Hyrule as well. She has incredible magic powers and a hunger for knowledge.

2 The King of Red Lions

Link's trusty talking boat in *The Wind Waker* is essential for navigating the Great Sea, but it has a secret identity.

3 Midna

A mysterious character from the Twilight Realm, Midna's fearsome attacks come in handy when she teams up with Wolf Link.

Latest game:
The Legend of Zelda: Breath of the Wild

Released:
2017

This massive adventure has Link exploring a vast, open-world Hyrule, building his strength and honing his skills before taking down the ancient evil of Calamity Ganon once and for all.

Abilities:
◆ Sword fighting
◆ Climbing
◆ Puzzle solving
◆ Horseback riding
◆ Sailing ◆ Archery

Triforce Wielder

Link is often associated with the Triforce of Courage, while Zelda and Ganon are tied to Wisdom and Power.

Hero with many voices

Several people have voiced Link, with actress Fujiko Takimoto lending her talents to the character in seven of the games.

Master swordsman

Though he's used many weapons over the years, Link's trademark is the legendary Master Sword, which first appeared in *A Link to the Past*.

A legend reborn

Most *Zelda* games feature a different version of Link, but all of them are linked through the mythical "spirit of the hero."

Link can traverse *Breath of the Wild's* Hyrule across land, sea, and air.

The graphics of *The Wind Waker* make Link look pretty adorable.

Top 5

Zelda games

Link's greatest adventures

Nintendo's classic adventure series spans more than 20 years and dozens of games, but which of them come out on top? Here we count down Link's best-ever outings.

Did you know?

The *Zelda* series has a complicated timeline that stretches across multiple parallel universes.

1

Breath of fresh air

The Legend of Zelda: Breath of the Wild

It's not just the biggest *Zelda* game ever, *BOTW* is the best, too. Whether gliding across Hyrule or battling inside a Divine Beast, its sense of adventure can't be beaten.

Top-down masterpiece

2

The Legend of Zelda: A Link to the Past

The best 2-D *Zelda* game, *ALTTP* still holds up. Filled with amazing moments, you'll never forget finding the Master Sword.

4 A dream to play

The Legend of Zelda: Link's Awakening

This handheld *Zelda* is underrated, but contains some of the best dungeons and puzzles in the series. Plus, it takes place in a fish's dream!

3 Timeless classic

The Legend of Zelda: Ocarina of Time

The first 3-D outing in the series, *Ocarina of Time* transformed *Zelda* games forever thanks to its music, iconic characters, and vast open spaces to explore.

5 High seas adventure

The Legend of Zelda: The Wind Waker

Not everyone was completely convinced with the cartoony art style that *Wind Waker* introduced, but the island-hopping adventure has since become one of the most beloved *Zelda* games ever.

? Q&A !

2-D or 3-D Zelda: which is better?

Both have their strong points. It's hard to beat the epic scale of the 3-D adventures, but while their graphics tend to age quickly, the 2-D games remain as gorgeous as ever.

What's the worst Zelda game?

A trio of *Zelda* games were released for the Philips CD-I console. They weren't made by Nintendo and most fans pretend they don't exist.

Get good at

Ooblets

Pokémon meets Animal Crossing

In this cute and colorful RPG, you look after a farm and collect adorable creatures called ooblets that you can do battle with to level them up. You can also grow crops, decorate your house, and go exploring to discover new ooblets.

Gaming secret

Where credit is due Fans that supported *Ooblets* on Patreon at the "Special Thanks" tier for $20 got their name in the game's credits as a reward.

Tips & Tricks

Go exploring
Different areas will have their own special plants, characters, and ooblets to discover.

Town planning
Completing quests and exploring will unlock new shops and buildings in town.

TOP 3
inspirations

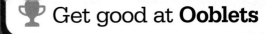

Pokémon

1 Developer Glumberland says that the *Pokémon* series is one of the game's main inspirations. Just like in *Pokémon*, there are loads of cool creatures to discover, each with their own abilities.

Did you know?
Ooblets was mostly made by a team of only two people: Rebecca Cordingley and Ben Wasser.

Animal Crossing

2 There are lots of characters to meet and interact with in *Ooblets*. This was inspired by the town-life simulation of the *Animal Crossing* series.

Harvest Moon

3 Looking after your land and farming crops is an important part of the game. This was partly inspired by the famous farming series, *Harvest Moon*.

Winter 25
12:35 PM
6,736.405G

Encyclopedia.

Lunch time

Feeding your ooblets the crops that you grow will help them level up and learn new moves.

Shop keeper

You can run your own shop where you sell produce you've farmed and junk you've found.

Get into
Sports games

Become a sports superstar

Sports games let you take control of your favorite teams and players, and become a sports legend without leaving home! Test your skills and make it to the top.

Retro roots

You can customize your character with clothes that you unlock in *Everybody's Golf.*

John Madden Football The first game in the *Madden NFL* series was one of the first huge sports game successes. *FIFA* and *Sensible Soccer* followed.

FIFA has a story mode called The Journey, where you play as rookie Alex Hunter.

QUICK TIPS

Rank up
Don't worry if you can't hit far at first in *Everybody's Golf.* Keep playing to level-up your clubs.

Finesse shot
Hold RB on Xbox One or R1 on PS4 to do an accurate finesse shot in *FIFA 18.*

TOP 3 GAMES

FIFA 18

1 *FIFA 18* is full of fun ways to enjoy soccer. You can play through cups and leagues, play against friends locally, play co-op online, or collect Ultimate Team cards to build your own dream team of the best players.

★ ★ ★ ★ ★ ★ ★ ★ ★ ★ ★ ★ ★ ★ ★ ★ ★ ★ ★ ★

NBA 2K18

2 *NBA 2K18* has a cool Career mode where you create your own player and play through the story of their basketball career. It's fun to create yourself and pretend you're a real basketball star.

★ ★ ★ ★ ★ ★ ★ ★ ★ ★ ★ ★ ★ ★ ★ ★ ★ ★ ★ ★

Everybody's Golf

3 This colorful golf game is easy to get into, with simple controls and easy holes to play. As you get better at the game, you can take on more difficult courses.

Hit hard

If you're in the sand in *Everybody's Golf*, then you need to hit harder than you normally would.

Mix It Up

Don't hold sprint all the time in *NBA 2K18*. Mix up your pace to trick the other team.

👍 If you liked these, try out

Tony Hawk's Pro Skater 5

Madden NFL 18

Football Manager 2016

Animal Crossing: Pocket Camp

squid

Tap and go!

A *nimal Crossing: Pocket Camp* brings the cute world of *Animal Crossing* from your Nintendo 2DS to your smartphone. Design your perfect campsite, pick out new outfits, decorate your campervan, and make friends with dozens of quirky animals.

Gaming secret

Magic money tree Each day, a random tree in *Pocket Camp* will drop bonus Bells if you shake it. And they say money doesn't grow on trees . . .

Tips & Tricks

Check the timers
Pocket Camp lets you know when fruit will grow back, so pay attention to the timers on each tree.

Craft amenities
Crafting amenities, like the treehouse and picnic set, will allow you to upgrade your friendship levels.

TOP 3
campsite pals

Apollo
1 If you want your camp to be the hippest around, then you need Apollo to visit. This cool customer might act like he doesn't care, but he's actually a sweetheart.

Chrissy
2 She might be a bit high maintenance, but Chrissy's worth it. She adores anything cute, so you'll want to craft some adorable furniture in order to keep her happy.

Did you know?
Since its launch, *Pocket Camp* has been downloaded more than 22 million times, and made more than $17 million worldwide.

big stripe
simple stripes
two-tone
horizontal stripes

Kid Cat
3 Part superhero, part sports nut, and all friendly feline, Kid Cat is a blast to have at your camp. His infectious personality and positive attitude should rub off on other guests too!

Reach your goals
Timed goals expire after a set period—complete them so you don't miss out on bonus rewards.

Browse the market
The stores in the market rotate regularly, so check back later if you don't see anything you like.

Awesome abilities

The coolest powers in gaming

One of the amazing things about video games is that they let you do some amazing and impossible things, like explore new worlds and run incredibly fast. Here are the best five gaming abilities of all time.

Did you know?

Kirby is a bit of a cheat when it comes to abilities. He can copy any ability, providing he eats the creature first.

1

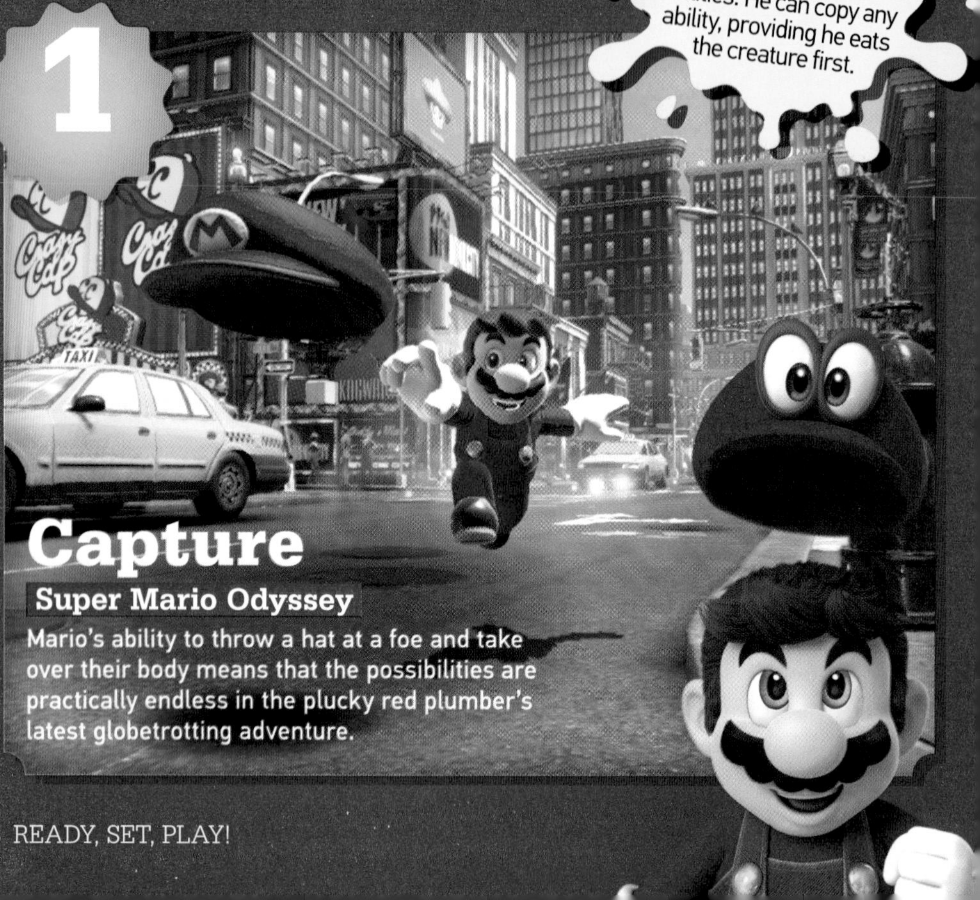

Capture

Super Mario Odyssey

Mario's ability to throw a hat at a foe and take over their body means that the possibilities are practically endless in the plucky red plumber's latest globetrotting adventure.

2

Samus' everything

Metroid series

Morph Ball? Power Bombs? Power Beam? Samus has it all. She may have these abilities thanks to her power suit, but we think she's just as dangerous outside of it, too.

3 Star surfing

Kirby series

Count on your fingers how many characters can *surf on a star*. Yeah, it's only Kirby. Star surfing helps Kirby perform some awesome moves and soar high into the air to get hard-to-reach items.

4 Relic absorption

Knack series

Knack's a plucky little hero to begin with, but he's got a whole lot of potential. He can add relics into his body to turn him from a three-foot scrappy fighter into a giant wrecking machine!

5 Sonic's speed

Sonic series

The blue blur is all about speed—be it running, spin-dashing, rail-grinding, or even piloting vehicles. And it's speed that makes Sonic a hedgehog to be reckoned with.

 ASK A PRO

Investigate the Action Guide if you ever forget any of Mario's moves in *Super Mario Odyssey*. You can find it in the Pause menu. The Action Guide will remind you how the controls work and what Mario's basic moveset is. It also helps you keep track of the different ways to capture Mario's enemies.

10
toughest
Achievements
& Trophies

These are for master gamers only!

2 The Impossible Dream

Steamworld Dig 2

While *Steamworld Dig 2* isn't the hardest game to play, the combination of requirements for this Trophy makes it a real challenge. To get it, you'll have to finish the game in under four hours, collect 100 percent of the items, have $15,000 in the bank, and not die once. Not quite impossible, but not far off!

1 On a Rail

Minecraft

This one is going to take *a lot* of patience. You have to travel at least 1,640 feet (500 meters) in one direction on a mine cart. You'll need to collect 18 gold bars, 186 iron bars, 34 sticks, and three Redstones to build the required 496 normal and 18 powered rails necessary to pull this off.

Celeste might start out easy enough, but its platforming challenges will quickly rise in difficulty level.

3 Massive Mythology

TowerFall Ascension

It's a good thing this is one of the best brawlers available on consoles, because this Achievement is unlocked only after you play a lot of the game. If you want this Trophy in your collection, you'll need to have 5,000 completed rounds!

4 Thanks For Playing

Celeste

Celeste is a test of skill and patien as it delights in twisting up your fi Nowhere is that more apparent t this Achievement, which require complete all hidden C-Sides—ch that are so impossibly difficult t take up hours of playtime.

One of the more difficult games to be released in recent years, *Cuphead* is a hyper-hard, boss-rush game with beautiful graphics!

5 Rolling Sixes
Cuphead

Cuphead is well-known for being a hard game that needs you to have quick reaction times. To earn this Achievement you must put everything you've learned to the test, beating final boss King Dice without taking a single hit. You'll need quick reflexes to win this one.

6 Mr. Perfect
Mega Man 10

This Trophy is technically achievable, but we still don't buy it. It requires you to beat *Mega Man 10*—another famously difficult game—without getting hit, not even once! You'd have to be a *Mega Man* magician to make it through without a scratch.

Mega Man games have always been known to be tricky, requiring great skill and quick

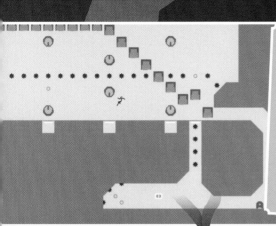

7 Platinum++
N++

This classic 2-D platformer has a big reputation for being super difficult. Not only do you need to quickly dodge spikes, bombs, missiles, and even more to achieve All-Gold medals, you'll have to do so across hundreds of different levels. It's practically impossible!

8 Trail Blazer
EA Sports Active 2

The requirement for this Achievement is simple—all you need to do is go on a run, tracked by *EA Sports Active 2*. The catch is that you'll need to run a whopping 621 miles (1,000 kilometers) to unlock it. That's almost as far as running from New York to Chicago—and back again!

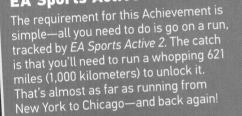

9 Didn't Miss a Beat
Strider

You'll need super reflexes to master this one. *Strider* makes you push all the way through to the Balrog battle at the end of the game, and you must defeat him on the first try. If you fail the first time, you'll have to restart the *entire game* to try for this again.

10 The King of New Rush City
SpeedRunners

A deceptively simple game, this tough Achievement tasks you with beating all chapters in the game on Unfair difficulty. The AI-controlled character you are racing moves faster, and makes zero mistakes. Fewer than one percent of players on Xbox One have managed to get this Achievement!

Get good at

Angry Birds

Fly with one finger

The *Angry Birds* series is nearly ten years old! It's a simple concept: you fling the birds at structures to take down the enemy pigs and protect your eggs. Add spells, abilities, and cool costumes, and you get one amazing game on your tablet or smartphone.

Gaming secret

Epic fail There is a cool Achievement in the game called Epic Fail. To earn this dubious Achievement, you need to launch ten birds in a row without popping any pigs.

Tips & Tricks

Daily bonuses
Completing these will earn you gems, which can be used for refilling lives or opening chests.

Level up
Collecting feathers will level up your bird. The higher the level, the bigger the scores they get.

TOP 3 Birds

Bomb

1 Bomb is great if you need to hit something hard. Just get him in the right place and tap the screen to blow him up! He can knock over anything.

Silver

2 Why attack from the side when you can hit from above? Launch Silver over a tower, then tap the screen since she's above, and watch her spin and dive down.

Did you know?

There are 2,500 levels in Angry Birds 2—more than double the amount in the original Angry Birds.

Red

3 Red is the best all-arounder in the game. As he flies toward the pigs' structures, you can activate his ability to let out a battle cry, shaking what is in front of him.

Scan the area

Zoom in and inspect the structures before launching any birds. A good plan always helps.

Strike!

If you can beat the area using just one bird, you will earn a cool bonus of 25,000 points.

Get to know

Kirby

Gaming's cutest character

No one really knows what the little pink blob called Kirby is, but we love him anyway. Kirby has been in loads of great platformers since his first game, *Kirby's Dream Land*.

Kirby's TOP 3 games

1 **Kirby's Epic Yarn**
In this platformer, Kirby is turned into yarn and sent to Patch Land, a world made of fabric.

2 **Kirby: Canvas Curse**
In this game you use a stylus to draw rainbow lines, and Kirby rolls along them like a ball.

3 **Kirby: Triple Deluxe**
Triple Deluxe has a cool 2.5-D design that lets you jump between foreground and background using Warp Stars.

Latest game:
Kirby Star Allies

Released:
2018

In Kirby's newest adventure, he can throw hearts at enemies to turn them to his side. Kirby can perform special attacks by working together with these new friends.

Abilities:
- Sucking up enemies
- Copying abilities
- Riding Warp Stars
- Jumping
- Floating
- Fighting
- Eating

Get to know **Kirby**

Big balloon
By taking a big gulp of air, Kirby can puff up like a balloon and float in the air.

The right attitude
Kirby has a cheerful personality, a positive attitude, and a love for all kinds of food.

Ready to rumble
Kirby appears alongside stars like Mario and Link in the fighting game *Super Smash Bros.*

Super sucker
Kirby is famous for being able to suck up enemies and copy their special skills.

Kirby has his own Dream Land stage in *Super Smash Bros.*

Kirby teams up with an ally to perform a powerful ice attack.

READY, SET, PLAY! **107**

Get good at

Kirby Star Allies

Chomping with friends

Kirby Star Allies is the latest addition to the long-running platforming series, and it's all about working with your friends to beat its many challenges and puzzles. As always, enemies can be swallowed to take their powers, and you can combine them to make extra special powers, too!

Gaming secret

A veteran Kirby has been around for over 26 years, and first appeared in Kirby's Dream Land on Game Boy in 1992. He's been in over 20 games. KSA is his first on Nintendo Switch.

Tips & Tricks

Foes are friends

Any enemy can become a friend! Just throw a heart at them.

Knock your combinations

Friends have different abilities, so experiment to see which ones work best.

TOP 3
bosses

Whispy Woods

1 No *Kirby* game would be complete without an appearance from the big, pink ball's most recognizable bad guy, so you'll be pleased/terrified to hear the evil tree is back for *KSA*.

Meta Knight

2 The other most recognizable villain on Kirby's naughty list is the sword-swinging Meta Knight. His boss stage includes clones of himself and flying boulders. Watch out!

Did you know?

Kirby keeps four of his most iconic moves for *KSA*, including Inhale, Star Spit, Slide Attack, and Air Gun. He'll be able to float, too.

Francisca

3 Meet one of *KSA*'s newest bosses. She's one of the three Mage Generals, and she's sometimes known as the Snow Flower.

Parasol shields

If you have a friend with a parasol, you can activate Chumbrella, which creates a big shield.

Know your bosses

Certain friends can make bosses a *lot* easier. A fire friend will help beat Whispy Woods.

Get good at

Forza Motorsport 7

Race to victory!

Race a supercar around the world's most famous tracks in *Forza Motorsport 7*. This realistic racer features more than 700 unlockable cars, from classic streetcars to modern F1 cars, and 32 global track locations to try out.

Gaming secret

Top speed The fastest recorded speed in the game is 274 miles per hour (440km/h), which was set by the 1956 Jaguar D-Type on the Old Mulsanne Le Mans track.

Tips & Tricks

Watch the skies
It might rain in the middle of a race. If it does, brake earlier when approaching corners to avoid skidding!

Rare cars
Check out the Specialty Dealer in the Car menu. You can buy rare cars, and might find a cool one.

TOP 3 coolest cars

Ford GT Forza Edition

1 This car was designed specifically for *Forza Motorsport 7*, and it's one of the fastest cars that Ford makes. Switch to the in-car camera and you'll feel like you're really driving it!

LaFerrari FXX K

2 This is the rarest car in the game, and can travel at a top speed of 214 miles per hour (344km/h)! We love the classic red Ferrari coloring.

Did you know?
The 1962 Ferrari 250 GTO is the most expensive car in the game—it costs more than $50 million!

Porsche GT2 RS

3 This Porsche was revealed alongside the game in 2017. It's one of only 131 cars in the game that can accelerate to over 200 miles per hour (321km/h), making it one of the fastest.

Feel the rumble

On acceleration, the right trigger of the controller vibrates to make it feel like the engine revving.

Follow the lines

If the arrows on the track turn red ahead, you must brake! Slow down until the arrows turn blue again.

Top 5
Wacky games
Weird and wonderful

Above all, gaming is about having fun. These games might sound strange, but they're hilarious—try them for yourself!

Did you know?

PaRappa the Rapper was first released in 1996 on the PlayStation and is thought to be the first true rhythm game.

1 Octodad

No one knows that Octodad is an octopus in human clothing! Help Octodad peform everyday activities, like grocery shopping, without blowing his cover.

2 Mario + Rabbids: Kingdom Battle

The raving rabbids of *Rayman* alone are pretty goofy, but add characters from *Mario* and you get nonstop jokes and wackiness. Just seeing personalities from both worlds interact is hilarious.

3 I Am Bread

That's right, you play as a piece of bread. You must move across the level and turn into toast while avoiding obstacles and without losing your edibility. It's weird, but strangely fun.

LOAF TOAST

4 PaRappa the Rapper

PaRappa uses beats and rhymes to solve his problems, from driving lessons to working at the flea market. His world is filled with odd characters, such as an onion man who teaches Kung Fu.

SCORE 7
BEST 0
TOUCHDOWN!

5 Touchdowners

It sounds simple: grab the ball and get to the opponent's endzone. However, your players' arms are constantly spinning, and passing the ball is wildly unpredictable.

ASK A PRO

There are plenty of quirky and cool games made for smartphones and tablets. A lot of these are free, too! Ask an adult to go into the App Store or Google Play and find the free apps. Check the age rating and then get permission to download it onto the device.

Get good at
Super Smash Bros.

Nintendo's battle royale

Nothing beats getting a cast of your favorite gaming characters together and pitting them against each other in a frantic fighting frenzy. *Super Smash Bros.* is over the top and can be pure chaos at times, but that's why it's so fun!

Gaming secret

Blast from the past You can unlock a variety of "Masterpieces" in *Super Smash Bros.* for Wii U. These are demos of the classic games in which the fighters made their names.

Tips & Tricks

Shields up
Some enemy attacks are unavoidable, but don't forget you can block with your shield at any time.

Toggle items
If you don't like a certain item, don't worry! *Smash Bros.* lets you customize which ones appear.

TOP 3
guest characters

Sonic

1 Sonic is a *Smash Bros.* veteran, having first turned up in *Brawl* on the Wii. His signature speed gives you an advantage in the arena.

Pac-Man

2 The classic arcade character is here to eat dots and do much more. He's even brought the famous *Pac-Man* ghosts along to help out in battle.

Did you know?
Super Smash Bros. for Wii U and 3DS have 58 playable characters, the most in the series to date.

Mega Man

3 Another old-school legend, Mega Man packs a real punch thanks to his arm cannon, which can produce a variety of attacks based on classic villains from the Capcom series.

Did you know?
In *Smash Bros.*, anyone can throw a Poké Ball to call a random Pokémon to their aid.

Find your favorite
Experiment with as many characters as possible. You never know which fighters you'll prefer.

Swap controllers
Smash Bros. supports lots of different control methods, so you can use the one that feels right.

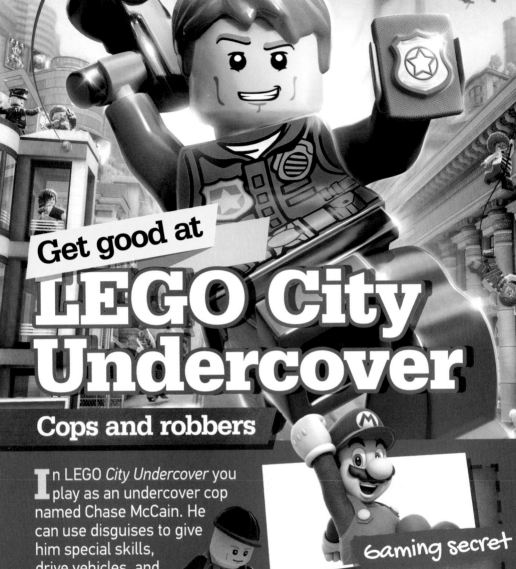

Get good at

LEGO City Undercover

Cops and robbers

In LEGO *City Undercover* you play as an undercover cop named Chase McCain. He can use disguises to give him special skills, drive vehicles, and use bricks to build things that will help him hunt down criminals.

Gaming secret

Mario undercover In the Nintendo versions of LEGO *City Undercover*, there are lots of hidden *Mario*-related items to find, like Warp Pipes and a Bullet Bill.

Tips & Tricks

Back to HQ
Remember to return to the police station to unlock the bonuses you have collected.

Go wandering
This is an open world game, so make sure you wander around to see what you can find.

TOP 3 LEGO remakes

LEGO Star Wars: The Force Awakens

1 LEGO *Star Wars: The Force Awakens* takes all the great characters and action from the movie and adds LEGO fun.

LEGO Harry Potter Collection

2 You can relive the school days of *Harry Potter* and his friends with this collection that brings together *Harry Potter Years 1-4* and *Harry Potter Years 5-7*.

Did you know?

LEGO *City Undercover* is set in an open world that you are free to explore in your hunt for criminals.

LEGO Jurassic World

3 This game takes the cool dinosaurs from the *Jurassic Park* series, and adds hilarious jokes and funny moments.

Smash stuff up

If you get stuck, try smashing everything around you. It will often help!

Red bricks first

Try to get red bricks first. They give you more points for the studs you collect.

Get into
World-building games

Creating your own place to play

World-building games are about your imagination. You can create amazing cities, huge castles, cool caves, and anything else you can dream up.

LEGO *Worlds* has some cool packs, like this space-themed one.

Retro roots

SimCity 2000 The *SimCity* series was a big influence on *Cities: Skylines*. The second game in the series, *SimCity 2000*, is one of the best.

Natural disasters can hit your city in *Cities: Skylines*, like this meteor.

QUICK TIPS

Build a shelter
Monsters come out at night in *Minecraft*, so build a shelter on your first day.

Plan your road
You should build a highway through your city in order to help the traffic flow in *Cities: Skylines*.

TOP 3 GAMES

Minecraft

1 *Minecraft* has been around for a while, but it's still one of the biggest games in the world. You can chop down trees and go mining for materials, craft your own tools, and then build things with your friends.

★★★★★★★★★★★★★★★★★★★★★★★★

Cities: Skylines

2 In this game, you are in charge of building your own city. Sandbox mode gives you the freedom to practice and experiment, and you don't have to worry about money.

★★★★★★★★★★★★★★★★★★★★★★★★

LEGO Worlds

3 In this fun LEGO world, you can find collectibles that give you "studs" to spend, fly around in helicopters, and—of course—use LEGO bricks to build your own amazing creations.

Discovery

Remember to use the Discovery tool when you get to a new area to copy things you can build.

👍 **If you liked these, try out**

SimCity Creator

Godus

Planet Coaster

Get to know

Yooka & Laylee

The best team in gaming

The cool chameleon, Yooka, and the wise-cracking bat, Laylee, are the perfect team. Each has its own special abilities, and when used together, they can overcome any challenge.

Yooka & Laylee's TOP 3 friends

1 Kartos
Yooka and Laylee can jump into their friend, Kartos, for some exciting rides on the minecart rails.

2 Trowzer
Trowzer the snake will sell Yooka and Laylee cool new abilities in exchange for the Quills you've collected.

3 Rextro Sixtyfourus
This lovable dinosaur lets you play lots of fun games on the arcade machines that he takes care of.

Latest game:
Yooka-Laylee
Released:
2017
In their debut adventure, Yooka and Laylee travel through some amazing levels together, collecting items, defeating enemies, and solving some pretty challenging puzzles.

Abilities:
- Lizard Leap
- Tail Twirl
- Sonar Shot
- Sonar Shield
- Air Attack
- Glide
- Camo Cloak

Get to know **Yooka & Laylee**

Personality clash
Yooka is easygoing and loves adventure. Laylee, on the other hand, loves mischief and is always cracking jokes.

Dynamic duo
Laylee rides on the back of Yooka, using her wings and special sonar powers to help him out.

Tongue tied
Yooka can shoot out his long, sticky tongue to grab objects like berries and butterflies.

Yooka and Laylee get on a slippery slide and enjoy the ride.

Roar power
Yooka was originally designed as a tiger, then a frog, before the game's developers decided on a chameleon.

With Laylee's wings you can glide after a jump, helping you cross big gaps.

 **FUN FACT**
Yooka and Laylee's names are a play on the name of the stringed instrument, the ukulele.

Get good at
Yooka-Laylee

A platformer packed with secrets

This awesome platformer is full of collectibles for you to find, and funny characters to meet as you explore its colorful world. You'll find yourself searching in every corner to discover all the secrets the game has hidden away.

Gaming secret

Squirreled away There is a book called *Jetpacks and Butlers* in the Archive area. This is a reference to another platforming hero: Conker the squirrel from the *Conker* games.

Tips & Tricks

Come back later
Revisit the game's early areas once you've unlocked new abilities, to get collectibles you've missed.

Don't rush
It's easy to fall off edges, especially in icy areas, if you try to go too fast.

TOP 3
bad guys

Capital B

1 Yooka-Laylee's biggest bad guy wants to steal all the world's books so he can make lots of money. You battle him at the end of the game to stop his evil plan.

Dr Quack

2 This dastardly duck is a scientist who makes inventions for Capital B, and creates an army of bad guys that you have to fight against.

Did you know?

Speedrunners have managed to finish Yooka-Laylee in less than 30 minutes!

Rampo

3 Rampo fires logs at you that you have to avoid to get close. Once you get to the boss, you must destroy his teeth to beat him.

Listen up

One hidden ghost can be found only by sound, so listen out for her giggling.

Equip the Hunter Tonic

The Hunter Tonic beeps when you're near something rare, helping you find hidden items.

Get good at
Slime Rancher

Build an awesome ranch

In *Slime Rancher*, your goal is to build up your ranch and fill it with colorful blobs called "slimes" that you can catch by sucking them up in your Vacpack. By feeding and breeding slimes, you earn cash to upgrade your ranch.

Gaming secret

Secret vaults Finish *Slime Rancher*, and three secret vaults with treasure inside will appear. You'll need to bust a Gordo to get a slime key and get inside to claim your treasure.

Tips & Tricks

Don't catch, shoot
If you're lucky enough to spot a gold slime, make sure you shoot it, and it will drop gold chunks.

Keep them separate
Keep different types of slimes separate, or they can cause chaos.

TOP 3 slimes

Pink slimes

1 These slimes will get you started. They won't cause any big problems on your ranch, and will help you learn how the game works before you start collecting more valuable slimes.

Puddle slimes

2 These rare slimes are great because they are so easy to take care of. They only eat water, so build them a little pool on your ranch, and you can start making some easy money.

Did you know?

New slimes to catch and areas to explore have been added to the game over time via free updates.

Tabby slimes

3 These cat-like slimes can cause a bit of trouble thanks to their love of stealing food, but they are the cutest slimes in the game. We love having them on our ranch.

Smash crates

Suck up crates with your Vacpack, and then smash them. You can find rare items inside.

Hose them down

You are able to get rid of angry Tarr slimes if you want to by shooting water at them.

Glossary

AI
"Artificial intelligence," the code used to make in-game characters behave as they do. It powers the enemies in nearly every game.

Achievement
An award you can unlock for completing a specific task on an Xbox console. This could include things like completing a level or beating a boss.

Beta
A small part of a game that the developers release early to let players test it. They use the tests to check that everything works properly.

Mini-games
Quick challenges within a video game that will earn you bonuses if you win. Some games, like *Mario Party*, are based around these.

Mob
Mobs are living game creatures that are affected by physics and can interact with players or other mobs. They are divided into various categories, such as Passive, Neutral and Hostile.

Boss
A tough enemy, usually found at the end of a level, that is bigger and more powerful than the normal enemies that appear. Bosses often have a weak point that can be targeted.

Local multiplayer
Playing a multiplayer game with other people in the same room. Games like *Mario Kart* have modes that let you play locally.

Mobile game
Games that are available to play on mobile devices, like smartphones and tablets.

Multiplayer
Multiplayer games and modes need multiple people to play them at once. They can be friends or others playing the same game.

Online multiplayer
Competing against other players via an Internet connection. You can add your friends to a list so you can play with them online.

Platformer
A type of video game that has you jumping across platforms to reach a final goal. 2-D platformers have players running from side to side, while 3-D platformers let you explore a full, 3-D world.

Power-up
Power-ups are objects that instantly benefit or add extra abilities to your character.

Rhythm game
The beat of the music gives you a hint of when to press a button or perform a move.

RPG
"Role-playing game," where you take on the role of a character and develop their skills.

Sandbox
Open-world games where players are free to play around and experiment however they wish—things like the Hub areas in LEGO games.

Trophy
An award you can unlock for completing a specific task on PlayStation consoles. Trophies come in bronze, silver, gold, and platinum, depending on their level of difficulty.

Unlockable
Items or abilities that become available to you as you progress. You can unlock these by reaching a new level, buying them with in-game money, or finding them hidden in the world.

World-building game
World-building games, like *Minecraft* and LEGO *Worlds*, give the ability to create your own worlds.

XP
Experience Points. Usually refers to in-game points that your character gains as you play. Earning a certain amount of points will cause your character to level up and become more powerful.